FAREWELL
to the Old House

THE METROPOLITAN OPERA HOUSE

1883—1966

Mrs. August Belmont, Founder and President Emeritus of the Metropolitan Opera Guild. From a portrait by Simon Elwes in the Guild Room at the Metropolitan.

FAREWELL
to the Old House

THE METROPOLITAN
OPERA HOUSE
1883–1966

Edited and Compiled by

STUART PRESTON

DOUBLEDAY AND COMPANY, INC. · GARDEN CITY, NEW YORK

Library of Congress Catalog Card Number 66-19363
Copyright © 1966 by Doubleday & Company, Inc.
All Rights Reserved
Printed in the United States of America
First Edition

Cover photo by Ralph Morse, Life Magazine, © Time, Inc.

TO ALL THOSE
WHO HAVE MADE
THIS HOUSE FAMOUS

SOUVENIR PROGRAM COMMITTEE

CO-CHAIRMEN   Mrs. Ogden Phipps
Mrs. Edmund C. Lynch, Jr.

MEMBERS   Mrs. August Belmont
Mrs. Lewis W. Douglas
Mrs. John DeWitt Peltz
Mr. Stuart Preston
Mr. Joseph A. Thomas
Mrs. John Barry Ryan

ACKNOWLEDGMENTS

In preparing this souvenir book of the Metropolitan Opera's farewell to its old house I have received nothing but courteous cooperation from the staff at the Metropolitan. My thanks go to **Opera News** and to the Metropolitan Opera Archives who have given me permission to reproduce photographs in their possession. I have taken great advantage of the knowledge and kindness of Mrs. John DeWitt Peltz, the opera's archivist. I am much indebted to Gerald Fitzgerald of **Opera News,** whose absorbing book **The Golden Horseshoe** (written in collaboration with Frank Merkling and John W. Freeman), explores the subject in depth. I also wish to thank my fellow members of the Souvenir Book Committee for their wise advice. Finally, to the friendship of Mrs. Ogden Phipps I owe a stimulus and encouragement which those who share it will alone appreciate.

S. P.

LIST OF ILLUSTRATIONS

SECTION I: *The Building 1883–1966*

1. The Opera House, 1884
2. An Opera House Ball, January 2, 1884
3. Architectural details, interior
4. Two story floor plan
5. Josiah Cleveland Cady
6. Burned-out stage, August 27, 1892
7. *Carmen,* August 27, 1892
8. *Faust,* circa 1900
9. Gala Performance for Prince Henry of Prussia
10. Street scene near the Opera, 1890s
11. Inaugural Night, October 22, 1883, Gounod's *Faust*
12. The Corps de Ballet, circa 1900
13. Christine Nilsson
14. Italo Campanini
15. Franco Novara
16. Sofia Scalchi
17. Augusto Vianesi
18. Skyscrapers and the Metropolitan
19. Italian Renaissance window
20. The great ceiling
21. Up from the parterre boxes
22. A riot of ornament
23. *Art nouveau* fountain
24. Special view of *Aida*
25. Frescoed *putti*
26. First night audience
27. *Entre'acte*
28. Rudolf Bing and Giulio Gatti-Casazza
29. Day ends

SECTION II: *The Curtain Falls*

30. Jean de Reszke
31. Emma Calvé
32. Marcella Sembrich
33. Nellie Melba
34. Enrico Caruso
35. Geraldine Farrar
36. Feodor Chaliapin
37. Antonio Scotti
38. Lucrezia Bori
39. Lotte Lehmann
40. Giovanni Martinelli
41. Ezio Pinza
42. Lauritz Melchior
43. Maria Jeritza
44. Kirsten Flagstad
45. Triumphal scene from 1908-09 *Aida*
46. *Aida* on farewell night April 16, 1966
47. Leonard Warren

SECTION III: *The Management*

48. Rudolf Bing
49. Reginald Allen
50. Francis Robinson
51. John Gutman
52. Herman E. Krawitz
53. Robert Herman

About the House

Nearly eighty-three years—October 22, 1883, to April 16, 1966—measure the lifetime of the Metropolitan Opera House, a span of days—and nights —exceeded in length of time by several European opera houses but by none in operatic glory. The walls of the venerable and dignified old building resound with the incomparable voices and orchestras of a past which sets a formidable challenge to the future.

Actually, the founding of the Metropolitan has more to do with American social and economic history than with purely artistic values. In the early 1880s New York was straining at many old barriers, well on its way to being the financial capital of the world as well as the hub of America's cultural wheel. Museums, libraries, and places of learning had been abundantly established in the metropolis since the end of the Civil War. But the opera—the roof and crown of cultural life in European capitals—had lagged behind and was still housed unpretentiously in the old Academy of Music on 14th Street and Irving Place, a quarter of the city gradually becoming unfashionable and out of the way as residential New York spread northward. Nor did it offer the kind of glamorous setting (not to speak of physical accommodations) that the newly powerful families— Astors, Vanderbilts, Millses, Belmonts, Goelets, and others—considered their due. They had experienced at first-hand the splendors of the new Opéra in Paris and they determined to rival them if possible. No one can fairly deny that they succeeded, building as they did, with the Metropolitan, the largest theatrical auditorium yet constructed in America and a house whose imposing character has impressed many generations of music lovers.

The project for a new opera was launched in 1880. By the next year, after the usual complications of financing and delays in finding a suitable site, the trapezoid block between 39th and 40th Streets bounded by Broadway and Seventh Avenue was decided upon. Following a competition to which four architectural firms submitted designs, the directors awarded the commission to Josiah Cleveland Cady, an architect who already had the American Museum of Natural History to his credit. Valuably assisted by his principal designer, Louis de Coppet Bergh, he set to work at once, using as his chief model London's Covent Garden and incorporating features from La Scala in Milan and the Opéra in Paris. By 1883 the building was completed, designed in the "early Italian Renaissance manner," but dismissed scornfully by conservative New Yorkers as "that yellow brewery uptown."

Nor did the interior arrangements fail to ruffle democratic and egalitarian feelings. Far and away the most conspicuous architectural feature of the house were the horseshoe circles of boxes from which the new leaders of society would for many a year proclaim their power. Numerous were those who echoed the sentiments expressed in a judgment passed on the structure by the New York **Evening Post** on the day after the opening. "From an artistic and musical point of view the large number of boxes in the Metropolitan is a decided mistake. But as the house was decidedly built for social purposes rather than artistic, it is useless to complain about this, or about the fact that the opportunity was not taken to make of the building itself an architectural monument of which the city might be proud." Be that as it may, the actual statistics made an impressive showing. The house had a seating total of 3045; its stage measured 86 feet deep by 101 wide, and it cost in all, building and site, no less than $1,732,478.71.

Shortly afterward, other critics made more sensible comments. Writing in **Harper's Monthly,** Montgomery Schuyler asserted that "it is safe to say that there is no theatre in which there are fewer bad seats in proportion to its size, nor any opera house in which the difference between the best and worst boxes is so small." Fair-minded observers admired the commodious auditorium, the excellent acoustics and the devices for eliminating fire hazards, the curse of so many opera houses throughout history, and which, alas, were neglected. As for the interior decoration, Cady instructed the Boston architect E. P. Treadwell to "avoid all tawdriness and garish display." The color scheme combined red and gold; ivory prevailed on the woodwork; the box fronts were gilded, and a huge painting of Apollo and the Muses crowned the proscenium arch.

If the Metropolitan had remained until the end as first conceived, its last visitors would be at a loss to recognize the interior of 1883. The disastrous fire of August 27, 1892 destroyed the stage and heavily damaged the auditorium and was the occasion of numerous renovations. Almost every subsequent year saw some structural change, most of them intended to improve seating arrangements or modernize the mechanics of the stage. In 1903 the interior received its final important redecoration, when the firm of Carrere & Hastings virtually transformed the auditorium, building a new proscenium arch, installing a huge sunburst chandelier, and in every way making the house more sumptuous according to the most lavish Edwardian standards. Few substantial changes took place after that, although alterations constantly went on in the interests of comfort, convenience, and theatrical effectiveness. But this is to anticipate.

The curtain on that far-away opening night in 1883 rose on Gounod's **Faust,** then a "modern" opera, hardly more than twenty years old, its composer still alive and working hard. Oddly enough, this opera which originated in France had, in the role of Marguerite, Christine Nilsson, a Scandinavian (the original Marguerite of the Paris premiere of 1859) and as the Mephistopheles, Franco Novara, an Englishman, and the opera was given in Italian. The occasion was a brilliant one, a challenge to which the Academy of Music rose bravely, holding its own opening night (**La Sonnambula)** simultaneously. Rival feelings ran high, Colonel Mapleson, the Academy's director, declaring that the Old Guard stood solidly behind him. "My audience," he pontificated, "is the **Faubourg St. Germain** of the town. My rival is supported, I understand, by a number of rich persons who want some new way of spending money." Supporting this diehard attitude, the critic of New York's **Dramatic Mirror** claimed that at the Metropolitan, "the Goulds and the Vanderbilts and that ilk, perfumed the air with the odor of crisp greenbacks. The tiers of boxes looked like cages in a menagerie of monopolists." But, screech, though the Academy's champions might, its day was over. It lingered on for three years, and then **Finis.** "I cannot fight Wall Street" said Colonel Mapleson, bitterly. The Metropolitan won hands down, and Madame Nilsson was presented with a gold wreath which, conveniently, "could also be worn as a girdle."

Thus, under the general management of Henry E. Abbey, an enthusiast for Italian and French opera, the first season got off musically to a good start. But not so financially. When the dismayed directors found out that Abbey had succeeded in losing $600,000, they replaced him with Leopold Damrosch, who, with his son Walter as assistant conductor, launched the great tradition of German opera at the Metropolitan. Soon Wagner was being produced as nowhere else outside of Bayreuth. Enthusiasm greeted this program on the part of all but the boxholders who preferred lighter and more diverting stuff. Nothing illustrates their boredom with the "Ring" more vividly than a notice posted in the boxes in January 1891. "Many complaints" it read, "having been made to the directors of the Opera House of the annoyance produced by the talking in the boxes during the performances, the Board requests that it be discontinued."

By the mid 1890s the Metropolitan reached musical heights which could easily stand comparison with the leading European houses. Casts included legendary stars such as the de Reszke brothers, Jean and Edouard; Emma Eames; Lillian Nordica; Pol Plançon; Ernst Van Dyck; Lilli Lehmann; and Marcella Sembrich, as well as many other supreme singers of that fortunate day. And soon they were to be joined by Melba and Caruso. Matching the vocal triumphs of the stage, the house itself on Monday nights presented a scene of almost barbaric splendor. The tradition of the "Diamond Horseshoe," its glitter not exaggerated, came into being, and a towering social peak was scaled on the occasion of a gala evening held in honor of Prince Henry of Prussia, the Kaiser's brother, on February 25, 1902. Smilax festooned the auditorium and clusters of electric lights blazed from the exterior of the building, on the top of which was poised a brilliantly illuminated replica of the Imperial yacht, **Hohenzollern.** Such manifestations of wealth and grandeur: the palatial house, the tiaras, and the trains dazzled the public, which gazed awestruck at the maroon velvet parterre boxes as if they were so many throne rooms. Even Henry James, that seasoned observer of pomp and circumstance, was impressed, commenting on "the general extravagant insistence on the Opera, which plays its part as the great vessel of social salvation, the comprehensive substitute for all other conceivable vessels," and stating further that "the Opera, indeed, as New York enjoys it, is worthy, musically and picturesquely, of its immense function."

Each triumph seemed to lead on to further triumphs, and as one star waned another waxed. There were setbacks and upsets as well. In 1897 the tenor Armand Castelmary died of heart failure in the arms of Jean de Reszke at the close of the second act of **Martha.** In January 1905 the bridge across which Carmen escapes in the first act collapsed under the weight of the troop of soldiers, plunging them, without serious consequences, onto the stage below. On April 18, 1906, the company, on tour, had the misfortune to find itself in San Francisco, the day of the great earthquake and fire, when and where all its scenery and costumes were lost. And in 1907 the elaborate and costly production of Richard Strauss's **Salome** so outraged conservative opinion that it had to be withdrawn from the repertoire after a single performance. Thundered the musical critic on the **Tribune:** "The reviewer should be an embodied conscience stung into righteous fury by the moral stench with which **Salome** fills the nostrils of humanity."

Let no one suppose that the Metropolitan Opera House has presented opera exclusively. In recent years visiting ballet companies have made their principal American appearances there, continuing a long tradition of dance in the house going back to 1908 when Isadora Duncan interpreted "The Dance of the Future" to a startled audience. Drama, too, has made notable contributions to the story of the Metropolitan. In 1888 Edwin Booth played Hamlet to Helena Modjeska's Ophelia; in 1905 Mrs. Patrick Campbell gave a reading there; in 1917, twenty-five years after her "positively farewell appearance in America," Sarah Bernhardt released the famous **voix d'or** in a scene from **Trilby** with Sir Herbert Beerbohm Tree; and in 1923, shortly before her death, the exquisite Eleonora Duse performed the leading role in Ibsen's **Lady from the Sea.** Other

15

unexpected occupants of that august stage play have been Yvette Guilbert (1906); Ethel Barrymore and Blanche Bates (1911); Al Jolson, Weber & Fields, and the Dolly Sisters (1912); Harry Lauder (1918); and, perhaps oddest of all, George Bernard Shaw, who held forth on the subject, "The Future of Political Science in America," on April 11, 1933. Truly, the Metropolitan is a house of many mansions.

An important event took place in 1908 with the formation of the Metropolitan Opera Company. Previously the stockholding ownership group, which retained the use of the thirty-five parterre boxes in lieu of rental, had leased the house to various opera managers, the latter being responsible for hiring the company and staging the productions. But in 1908 the newly formed Metropolitan Opera Company took over direct control and appointed a general manager on a salary. Their first choice was a happy and memorable one, the Italian impresario Giulio Gatti-Casazza, who was to reign ably over the opera's affairs until his retirement in 1935. The year 1908 also marks the important election to the Presidency of the Board of Otto H. Kahn, a distinguished banker and princely patron of the arts, who wisely governed the opera until 1932.

Gatti brought with him to the Metropolitan his brilliant colleague at La Scala, Arturo Toscanini, who was to conduct there until 1915. Their first major joint effort was the world premiere of Puccini's **La Fanciulla del West,** starring Emmy Destinn and Enrico Caruso, an occasion attended by the composer himself who called the production "perfect." However, Gatti did not limit himself to the European repertoire. His long regime was responsible for the production of many American works.

Needless to say, World War I had a major impact on the fortunes of the opera. A number of Wagnerian singers withdrew from the company, and during the season of 1917-18 no German operas were given, and were not resumed until an English version of **Parsifal,** presented in 1920, broke the ice. On March 22, 1919, the twenty-fifth anniversary of Caruso's operatic debut in Italy was celebrated with a gala evening, an event more closely foreshadowing his final appearance there than his admirers realized. He sang for the last time in **La Juive,** at the Metropolitan on December 24, 1920, returning to Italy the next year to die at the age of forty-eight.

Notwithstanding this heavy loss, the Metropolitan maintained its high standards in the years between the two World Wars. The great stars of that period were Geraldine Farrar, Lucrezia Bori, Rosa Ponselle, Amelita Galli-Curci, Lotte Lehmann, Maria Jeritza, Antonio Scotti, Lawrence Tibbett, Giovanni Martinelli, Ezio Pinza, Grace Moore, Beniamino Gigli, and Giuseppe de Luca. During Gatti's final season he struck gold in the person of Kirsten Flagstad, whose glorious performances when teamed with Lauritz Melchior restored the Wagnerian repertoire to immense popularity. These years also saw the addition of a vast new public for the Metropolitan with the advent of radio broadcasts in 1940, sponsored by the Texaco Company.

As did many institutions largely dependent on public support, the Metropolitan suffered gravely from the great Depression of the early 1930s. Its very existence was threatened, and it might have gone under, at least temporarily, had it not been for the efforts of a campaign to raise funds for its survival. Headed by Lucrezia Bori, the committee got together $300,000, thus averting disaster. The next important step in the Metropolitan's history took place in 1940 under the management of Edward Johnson. In that year a nation-wide campaign raised $1,057,000. from the 166,000 donors in order to purchase the house from the stockholders. This marked the end of an era. On Johnson's retirement, he was succeeded as general manager by Rudolf Bing, who has brilliantly guided the Metropolitan's fortunes until the present, and who will preside over both the farewell to the old house and the herculean task of moving the opera to its new home in Lincoln Center.

In the words of Mrs. August Belmont, the distinguished and wise President Emeritus of the Metropolitan Opera Guild, "A toast to the Opera's glorious past, a salute to its magnificent future. And now, up with the curtain!" **Le Roi est mort. Vive le Roi!**

SECTION I

The Building 1883-1966

1. An early photograph of the Metropolitan, taken in 1884, a year before the telegraph poles were removed. (Opera News)

2. The Opera House on January 2, 1884, when a ball was given there for charity. (Opera News)

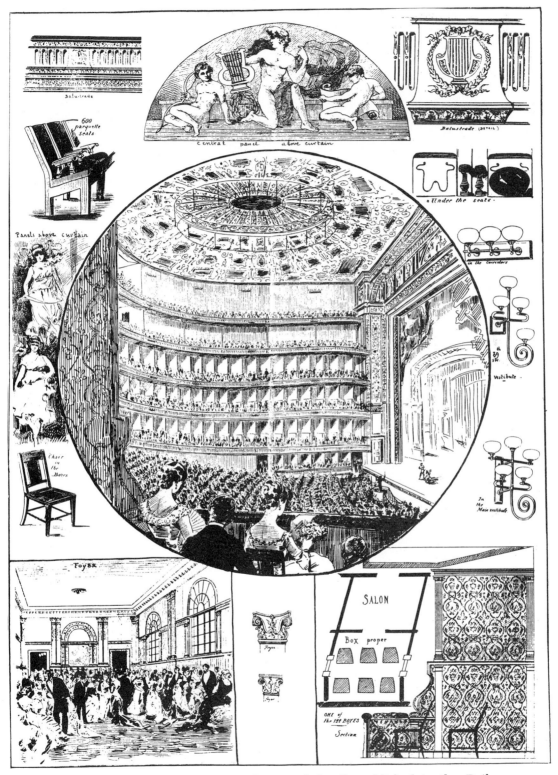

3. Drawings of the interior and of architectural details published in the *Daily Graphic* the morning after the opening. (Opera News)

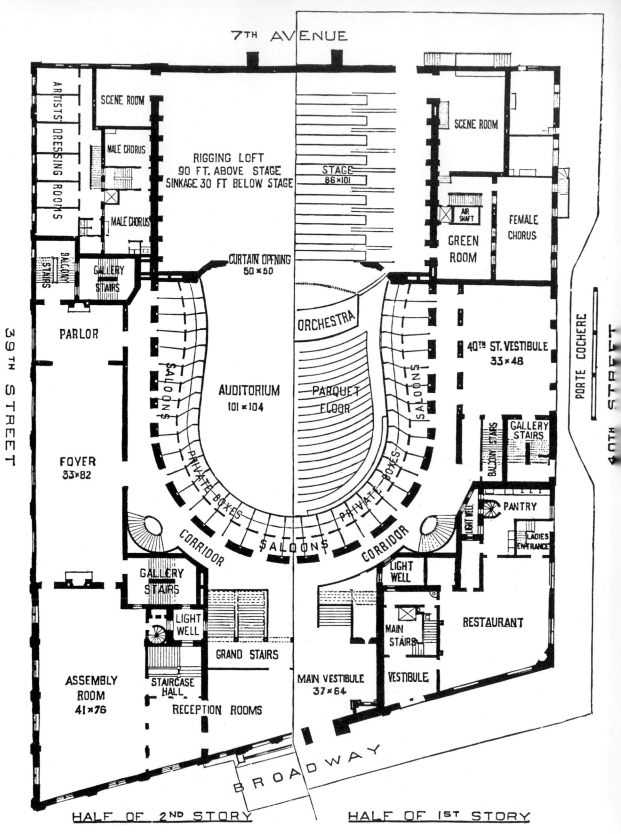

4. Floor plan showing two stories of the original Metropolitan.

5. Josiah Cleveland Cady, the architect of the Metropolitan Opera House.

6. Disaster strikes. The auditorium and the burned-out stage on the morning after the fire, August 27, 1892. (Metropolitan Opera Archives)

7. The Opera House restored. A high view of *Carmen* as staged in the late 1890s. (Metropolitan Opera Archives)

8. A rapt audience watches the apotheosis of Marguerite in the closing scene of
   Faust, circa 1900. (Metropolitan Opera Archives)

9. A Gala Opera Performance was held for Prince Henry of Prussia at the Metropolitan on February 25, 1902. (Opera News)

10. Streetcars, hansoms, and a single brougham on Broadway near the Metropolitan in the 1890s. (Metropolitan Opera Archives)

STEINWAY & SONS'

PIANO-FORTES.

THE STANDARD PIANOS OF THE WORLD.

Warerooms, Steinway Hall,

No. 107, 109 and 111 East Fourteenth Street,

NEW YORK CITY.

Park & Tilford,

917 and 919 Broadway,

656-660 Sixth Avenue.

118, 120, 122 Sixth Avenue,

NEW YORK.

— AND —

39 Rue de Chateau d'Eux,

PARIS.

RUNKEL BRO'S
FINE VANILLA
CHOCOLATE

C. F. KLUNDER,
FLORIST,
No. 907 BROADWAY, NEW YORK.

(Bet. 20th and 21st Sts.)

Lockadian Gardens at Sing Sing.

ARTISTIC
GAS FIXTURES,
Portable Stands, Fine Lamps,

OXLEY, GIDDINGS & ENOS,
224-230 CANAL STREET,

(3 Blocks East of Broadway)   NEW YORK.

METROPOLITAN
OPERA HOUSE.

MR. HENRY E. ABBEY, - - - - - - Director.
Acting Manager, - - - - - MR. MAURICE GRAU.

MONDAY EVENING, OCTOBER 22, 1883,

INAUGURAL NIGHT

AND

First Night of the Subscription,

WHEN GOUNOD'S OPERA OF

"FAUST."

Will be presented with the following Cast:

FAUST, - - - - - Sig. ITALO CAMPANINI
MEPHISTOPHELES, - - - Sig. FRANCO NOVARA
VALENTINO, - - - Sig. GIUSEPPE DEL PUENTE
WAGNER, - - - - - - - Sig. CONTINI
SIEBEL, - - - - - - Mme. SOFIA SCALCHI
MARTA, - - - - - Mlle. LOUISE LABLACHE
(Who has kindly consented to assume the part at short notice. Her first appearance.)

AND

MARGHERITA, - - - - Mme. CHRISTINE NILSSON

Musical Director and Conductor, · Sig. VIANESI

WEBER PIANO USED.

Mason & Hamlin's Organ Used.

All the above Operas performed at this House can be had in every form, Vocal and Instrumental
at G. SCHIRMER, No. 35 Union Square, Importer and Publisher of Music.

The Scenery by Messrs. Fox, Schaeffer, Maeder, and Thompson.
The Costumes are entirely new, and were manufactured at Venice by D. Ascoli
The Appointments by Mr. Bradwell.
Machinists, Messrs. Lundy & Gifford.

NIGHTLY PRICES OF ADMISSION:

Boxes, holding six (6) seats... $50
Orchestra Stalls... 6
Balcony Stalls.. 3
Family Circle (reserved)... 2
Admission to Family Circle... 1

Seats and Boxes can be secured at the Box Office of the Metropolitan Opera House, which
will remain open daily from 8 A. M. to 5 P. M.

Doors open at 7.15.   **Performances at 8 precisely**

Gunerius Gabrielson & Son, Florists to the Metropolitan Opera House.

Opera Glasses on Hire in the Lobby.

L. F. Mazette, Caterer.

Parties desiring Ices can be supplied by the Waiter, in Corridor.

Business Manager - - - - - - - - - Mr. W. W. TILLOTSON.
Treasurer - - - - - - - - - Mr. CHAS. M. MATHEWS.

Wm. Knabe & Co.

PIANO-FORTES.

UNEQUALED IN

Tone, ∴ Touch, ∴ Workmanship
and ∴ Durability.

WILLIAM KNABE & CO.,

No. 112 Fifth Ave.,

NEW YORK.

1789 Bacon Pianos. 1883

FRANCIS BACON'S PIANO FACTORY,

Late Raven & Bacon—Bacon & Karr.

Grand, Square and Upright Pianos,

BROADWAY and 42d STREET.

RICHARD HECKSCHER, Jr.

COAL.

OFFICES;

Trinity Building, 111 Broadway,

435 East 23d Street,

201 East 14th Street,

(Bet. 2d & 3d Aves.)

WHARVES;

Foot of 23d Street, East River.

Foot of Rivington, St.,   "

NEW YORK.

MITCHELL, VANCE & CO.,

Manufacturers of

Gas Fixtures, Lamps, Clocks

AND BRONZES,

836 and 838 Broadway, New York.

BARRETT HOUSE,

BROADWAY AND 43d STREET, - NEW YORK.

(European Plan).

Rooms, $1.00 Per Day and Upwards.

Wedding and Supper Parties a Specialty.

BARRETT BROTHERS,   Proprietors.

Steinway & Sons' Pianos are endorsed by Wagner, Rubenstein, Liszt, Theo. Thomas, Berlioz, etc.

11. Program of the Metropolitan's Inaugural Night, October 22, 1883, when Gounod's *Faust* was presented. (Metropolitan Opera Archives)

12. A rest period for the ballet at the Metropolitan, circa 1900.

13. "There is no resisting" Christine Nilsson as "Goethe's sweet child" wrote a critic after the first performance of *Faust*. (Metropolitan Opera Archives)

14. Italo Campanini sang the role of Faust on the opening night. (Opera News)

15. Franco Novara was diabolically magnetic in the role of Mephistopheles. (Metropolitan Opera Archives)

16. Sofia Scalchi had long impressed audiences with her graceful performance in the role of Siebel. (Metropolitan Opera Archives)

17. The conductor Augusto Vianesi
was at the podium on the night
of October 22, 1883.
(Metropolitan Apera Archives)

18. Once dominating its neighbors the Metropolitan ended by being towered over by
skyscrapers. (Serge le Blang)

19. A little-noticed window in the manner of the early Italian Renaissance (Alexandre Georges)

20. The great gold ceiling of the Metropolitan, Edwardian style at its most sumptuous. (Alexandre Georges)

21. Looking up from the
    parterre boxes to the ceiling.
    (Alexandre Georges)

22. A riot of sculptured gold
    plaster where box and
    proscenium meet.
    (Alexandre Georges)

23. Refreshment from an *art nouveau*
    fountain in the orchestra corridor.
    (Alexandre Georges)

24. A view of the triumphal scene in *Aida* that the audience never sees. (Gjon Mili)

25. Frescoed *putti* disport
    themselves on the ceiling
    above the Grand Tier foyer.
    (Alexandre Georges)

26. A first-night audience in search of celebrities. (Gjon Mili)

28. Past and present. Rudolf Bing not overshadowed
by the bust of his great predecessor, Giulio Gatti-Casazza.
(Gjon Mili)

27. A busy entre'acte

29. Now the day is over, Night is drawing nigh. (Gjon Mili)

The Curtain Falls

FAMOUS STARS IN THE ROLES IN WHICH THEY MADE THEIR FAREWELL OPERATIC APPEARANCES AT THE METROPOLITAN

30. Jean de Reszke made his Metropolitan debut in 1891 and sang a last Lohengrin on April 29, 1901. (Metropolitan Opera Archives)

left
31. Emma Calvé made her Metropolitan debut in 1893 and sang a last Carmen on March 2, 1904. (Metropolitan Opera Archives)

right
32. Marcella Sembrich made her Metropolitan debut in 1883 and sang a last Rossini in *The Barber of Seville* on February 6, 1909. (Metropolitan Opera Archives)

33. Nellie Melba made her Metropolitan debut in 1893 and sang a last Violetta in *La Traviata* on November 29, 1910.

34. Enrico Caruso made his Metropolitan debut in 1903 and sang a last Eleazar in *La Juive* on December 24, 1920. He is shown here with Rosa Ponselle in the role of Rachel. (Metropolitan Opera Archives)

35. Geraldine Farrar made her Metropolitan debut in 1906 and sang a last Zaza (in the opera of that name) on April 22, 1922. (Metropolitan Opera Archives)

36. Feodor Chaliapin made his Metropolitan debut in 1907 and sang a last Boris Godunov on March 14, 1929. (Opera News)

37. Antonio Scotti made his Metropolitan debut in 1899 and sang a last Chim-Fen in
    L'Oracolo on January 20, 1933. (Metropolitan Opera Archives)

38. Lucrezia Bori made her Metropolitan debut in 1912 and sang a last Manon on March 29, 1936. (Carlo Edwards)

39. Lotte Lehmann made her Metropolitan debut in 1934 and sang a last Marschallin
in *Der Rosenkavalier* on February 23, 1945. (Metropolitan Opera Archives)

left

40. Giovanni Martinelli made his Metropolitan debut in 1913 and sang a last Pollione in *Norma* on March 8, 1945. (A. Lavoisa)

right

41. Ezio Pinza made his Metropolitan debut in 1926 and sang a last Don Giovanni on March 5, 1948. (Muriel Frances)

42. Lauritz Melchior made his Metropolitan debut in 1926 and sang a last Lohengrin on February 2, 1950. (Constance Hope)

43. Maria Jeritza made her Metropolitan debut in 1921 and sang a last Rosalinde in *Die Fledermaus* on February 22, 1951. (Serge LeBlang)

44. Kirsten Flagstad made her Metropolitan debut in 1935 and sang a last Alceste on April 1, 1952. (Serge Le Blang)

45. Triumphal scene from *Aida* as presented at the Metropolitan Opera House during the 1908-09 season starring Emmy Destinn, Louise Homer, Enrico Caruso, Antonio Scotti and Adamo Didur, and conducted by Arturo Toscanini.

46. Triumphal scene from *Aida* as presented on the Metropolitan farewell night, April 16, 1966.

47. Leonard Warren bows to the house after a performance of Macbeth.

SECTION III

The Management

Metropolitan Opera Association Incorporated

OFFICERS

Lauder Greenway, *Chairman of the Board*
Lowell Wadmond, *Vice-Chairman of the Board*
Anthony A. Bliss, *President*
Floyd W. Jefferson, Sr., *Vice-President*
Mrs. Lewis W. Douglas, *2nd Vice-President*
Charles M. Spofford, *Chairman, Executive Committee*
George S. Moore, *Treasurer*
Gordon M. Hill, *Assistant Treasurer*
Reginald Allen, *Special Assistant to the President and the General Manager*
Herman E. Krawitz, *Secretary*
Lauterstein and Lauterstein, *Legal Counsel*
Robert N. Stringer, *Comptroller*

BOARD OF DIRECTORS

Mrs. August Belmont
  Emeritus Director
Anthony A. Bliss
Millard J. Bloomer, Jr.*
Walker G. Buckner
Owen Cheatham
Mrs. Lewis W. Douglas
John W. Drye, Jr.
J. William Fisher
Julius Fleischmann*
Mrs. Wm. Francis Gibbs
Francis Goelet
Lauder Greenway

Stanley Hawks
Gordon M. Hill
Howard J. Hook, Jr.
Kenneth Ives
Floyd W. Jefferson, Sr.
William J. Keary
Robert Lehman
Augustus C. Long
George S. Moore
Francis F. Randolph*
Mrs. John D. Rockefeller, Jr.
William Rockefeller
Mrs. John Barry Ryan

Grant G. Simmons, Jr.
Dr. Carleton Sprague Smith
Charles M. Spofford
Roger L. Stevens
Benjamin Strong
Frank E. Taplin
Langdon Van Norden
Royall Victor, Jr.
Lowell Wadmond
Mrs. Paul Felix Warburg
Mrs. Frederick K. Weyerhaeuser
Mrs. Charles B. Wrightsman

MEMBERS OF THE ASSOCIATION

Mrs. Vincent Astor
Talcott M. Banks
Roger M. Blough
Frederic Brandi
H. S. M. Burns
Mrs. Louis S. Cates
Mrs. Harold N. Cooledge
Mrs. J. Cheever Cowdin
Howard S. Cullman
Frederic G. Donner
Frank Donovan
Thomas M. Evans
Mrs. Anne McDonnell Ford
Michael V. Forrestal
Mrs. Polk Guest

Augustin S. Hart
Henry Townley Heald
Mrs. Gilbert Humphrey
James Jaffray
Arthur Kramer, Jr.
Mrs. Albert D. Lasker
Mrs. Alexander M. Laughlin
Leon Lauterstein
Albert A. List
John D. Lockton
Richard P. Loftus
Henry P. McIlhenny
Philip L. Miller
Malcolm Muir
Mrs. Allen G. Oliphant

Mrs. John DeWitt Peltz
Bernard Peyton
Clifton W. Phalen
Mrs. Ogden Phipps
Mrs. Brooks Potter
William Schuman
Howard C. Sheperd
Harvey M. Spear
Cornelius V. Starr
John P. Stevens, Jr.
Vernon Stouffer
Lewis L. Strauss
Mrs. Edgar Tobin
C. V. Whitney
Mrs. Theodore O. Yntema

ADMINISTRATION

Rudolf Bing *General Manager*
John Gutman, Robert Herman, Francis Robinson, Herman E. Krawitz *Assistant Managers*
George Schick *Music Consultant*
Paul Jaretzki *Assistant Artistic Administrator*
Frank Paola *Company Manager and Musical Secretary*
Glen Sauls *Assistant to the Artistic Administrator*
Charles Riecker, Michael Bronson *Assistant Technical Administrators*
Alfred F. Hubay *Box Office and House Manager*
Sol Wallace *Box Office Treasurer*
Henry A. Fischer *Assistant Comptroller*

* and the members of the Board of Directors except those indicated above by an asterisk

Metropolitan Opera

CONDUCTORS

Kurt Adler
Franz Allers
Karl Böhm
Fausto Cleva

Zubin Mehta*
Francesco Molinari-Pradelli*
Georges Prêtre

Joseph Rosenstock
George Schick
Thomas Schippers
Silvio Varviso

ASSOCIATE CONDUCTORS   Jan Behr, Martin Rich, Ignace Strasfogel

ASSISTANT CONDUCTORS

Julius Burger
Lawrence L. Smith

Walter Taussig
Umberto Vedovelli

William Weibel
Richard Woitach

Millard Altman, Gildo DiNunzio *Apprentice Conductors*
David Stivender *Assistant Chorus Master*
Adriano Petronio *Prompter*
Orchestra Manager Felix Eyle
Rehearsal Assistants and Coaches Alberta Masiello, Louise Sherman
Concert Master Raymond Gniewek

PRODUCTIONS STAGED BY

Yoshio Aoyama
Jean-Louis Barrault*
Henry Butler
Herbert Graf

Joseph L. Mankiewicz
Nathaniel Merrill
Günther Rennert
Cyril Ritchard

Margherita Wallmann
Margaret Webster
Dino Yannopoulos
Franco Zeffirelli

STAGE DIRECTORS   Ralph Herbert, Bodo Igesz, Richard Pearlman, Patrick Tavernia

PRODUCTIONS DESIGNED BY

Horace Armistead
Eugene Berman
Attilio Colonnello
H. M. Crayon
Jacques Dupont*

Frederick Fox
Rolf Gérard
Rudolf Heinrich
Leo Kerz

Ita Maximowna
Motley
Motohiro Nagasaka
Robert O'Hearn
Franco Zeffirelli

METROPOLITAN OPERA BALLET

Alicia Markova, *Director*   Audrey Keane, *Ballet Mistress*   Irving Owen, *Rehearsal Assistant*

ADMINISTRATIVE AND TECHNICAL STAFF

Clare Moroney, *Subscription Secretary*
Glenn B. Hill   } *Assistant House*
Norman Christensen } *Managers*
Harry G. Schumer, *Librarian*
John Grande, *Assistant Librarian*
William C. Brinkop, *Advertising*
William J. Harris, *Asst. Box Office Treasurer*
Charles B. Allen, *Libretti*
Arge Keller, *Rehearsal Department*
Merle Hubbard, *Rehearsal Department*
Dr. William G. MacDonald, *Medical Director*
Dr. Adrian Zorgniotti, *Asst. Medical Director*
Mary E. O'Connor, *Company Nurse*
Louis Edson, *Master Mechanic*
Rudolph Kuntner, *Chief Electrician*
George Fitzpatrick, *Chief Usher*

Warren Lawrence, *Scenery Construction*
Frank Smith, *Chief Engineer*
Richard Hauser, *Master of Properties*
Vladimir Odinokov, *Scenic Artist*
Maureen Ting, *Head Costumer*
Nina Lawson, *Hair Stylist and Wigs*
George Shindhelm, *Makeup Artist*
James Pinto, *Assistant Makeup Artist*
Rose Calamari, *Wardrobe Supervisor*
Charles Caine, *Wardrobe Coordinator*
Richard Graham, *Properties Construction*
Thomas Hillary, *Assistant to the*
Technical Administrator
Andrew Davidson }
Charles Bonheur } *Production Assistants*
Jay Rutherford }

STAGE MANAGEMENT

Osie Hawkins, *Executive Stage Manager*   Etienne Barone, *Stage Manager*
Stanley Levine, *Associate Stage Manager*

PRESS DEPARTMENT

Francis Robinson, *Press Director*
Anne Gordon }
Dale Heapps } *Associate Press Representatives*

Jeanne Thomas }
William Greenblatt } *Press Assistants*
Louis Mélançon, *Official Photographer*
Les Carr, *Assistant Photographer*

Mrs. John DeWitt Peltz *Archivist*   Marietta Fuller *Assistant to the Archivist*
Ione Page *Development Program Administrator*

*New Artist

48. Rudolf Bing, General Manager.

left
49. Reginald Allen, Special Assistant to the President and the General Manager.
     (Louis Mèlancon)

right
50. Francis Robinson, Assistant Manager

left
51. John Gutman, Assistant Manager (Louis Mèlancon)

right
52. Herman E. Krawitz, Assistant Manager. (Louis Mèlancon)

53. Robert Herman, Artistic Administrator. (Louis Mèlancon)